About Us

Jack M. Offman, "Best Selling" Author

Jack M. Offman, the undiscovered gem of questionable children's novels, is a 40-something who finds joy in the nerdy realm of laser tag and video games—probably why he's still single. While his books might often get the silent treatment, he passionately dives into them after introspective beach walks and avoiding DUIs. And for the record, he's the kind of guy who'd never risk a sprint with scissors. Legends say his zest for life might just be infectious, if anyone bothered to listen.

Anita V. Gina, God's Gift to Illustration

Anita V. Gina, a vivacious 20-something illustrating sensation, is certain she's the glitzy sequin in the artsy universe. Fully convinced that her fingers drip 24-karat magic, she's taken on the brave challenge of converting Jack M. Offman's poetic trainwrecks into bestsellers because, let's face it, she thinks he's about as artistic as a soggy... you get it. Though schooled in the classics, she's confident that her art game is so tight, Picasso might've begged her for a masterclass. Her dating profiles? The stuff of legends! But bafflingly, she's still single, always swiping left, wondering, "Why can't these dudes level up to my grandmaster canvas?"

Cleveland Steamer Press, Trash Book Publisher

Ah, Cleveland Steamer Press – surprisingly not from Cleveland and inspired by something so unsavory, we dare not speak its name. This publishing marvel somehow attracts authors even a garbage disposal might reject. Continually defying economic logic (never having turned a profit), this powerhouse pumps out "children's books" so dubious they're on society's blacklist. Truly, their books are best reserved for foes – consider them a paperweight with a vendetta.

WILLIE THE ENGINEER'S

MASSIVE ERECTIONS

A POETIC JOURNEY THROUGH ENGINEERING'S HARDEST FEATS

Jack M. Offman & Anita V. Gina

Hello there! Come closer! I'm Willie, that you see,
An Engineer, with experience, and as skilled as one can be.

Through history's lens with erections, I'll soon for sure reveal,
I'll share about some great big walls and spires made of steel.

Hardwood beams that straddle, and hefty pipes that lay,
Through bushes of ancient times, to pristine modern day.
Let's thrust into a journey, with heavy stones revealed,
A throbbing tale of glory, dripping with appeal!

It's time! Let's begin, to embark on our faithful quest.
I'll expose you to many erections, with vigor and with zest!

The Great Pyramid of Giza
Egypt, 2580 BC

In Egypt's hot sands, a vast structure was built,
Massive stones, erected tall, without any tilt.
Guarded by a big lion with a stoic man's face,
Deep inside her a crypt, through a sacred maze.
Her mystic inner chambers, secretive and deep,
Where only the boldest, have ever dared to creep.
Royalty was smart, with a twinkle in their eye,
They wrapped their beloved, before sticking them inside.

The Great Wall of China
China, 221 BC

For miles and miles and miles, a sprawling wall does go,
Over China's mountains high, deep through her valleys low.
Built so long ago, to keep her foes away,
In China's, it stands fully erect, to this very day.
Men risked their lives to summit her and failed,
It took a man named Genghis to scale, nail, and impale!
So to those who say that Chinese pipes are so small,
May think twice after seeing this Great Wall.

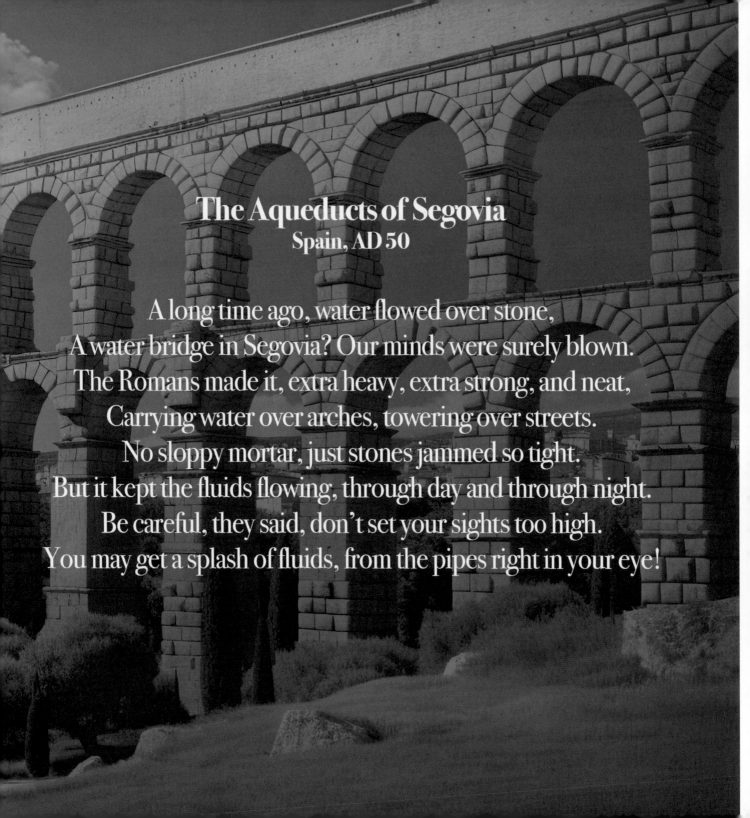

The Aqueducts of Segovia
Spain, AD 50

A long time ago, water flowed over stone,
A water bridge in Segovia? Our minds were surely blown.
The Romans made it, extra heavy, extra strong, and neat,
Carrying water over arches, towering over streets.
No sloppy mortar, just stones jammed so tight.
But it kept the fluids flowing, through day and through night.
Be careful, they said, don't set your sights too high.
You may get a splash of fluids, from the pipes right in your eye!

The Colosseum
Italy, 80 AD

In Rome, the Colosseum, her oval glory did stand,
Despite bloodflow heavy, men yelled, they came, they crammed!
With every thrust of sword, with every man to fall,
One would enter eager, to heed her center's call.
It once held 50,000, roaring with delight.
Can you imagine that carnal day, what a mortal sight!
Even though she is now shut up, and closed down so tight,
Can you imagine being inside her, even for just one night?

The Taj Mahal
India, 1653

A big white palace, shiny and bright,
Made for a queen, in India's light.
Standing so pretty, like a dream,
Curved shafts surrounded, her swollen domes gleam.
It took 20 years to completion, to make it just right.
It didn't come too early, with 20,000 men's might.
A river runs by, ebbing and flowing,
And people never stop, coming and going.

The Brooklyn Bridge
USA, 1883

A bridge in New York, so fine and so tall,
Connecting people and places, both big and small.
Her foundations jammed deep, where bedrock does lay,
A popular route, folks ride her each day.
Made from steel and stone, her parts do bind tight,
An erection over water, a master of mind.
With the weight of the world, pulling on her shoulders,
She can flex with the wind, but never bends over.
Connecting two boroughs, through this expansive endeavor,
And people keep coming, forever and ever.

The Eiffel Tower
France, 1889

In Paris, a magnificent tower does rise,
Stroking the clouds, and thrust into the skies.
Her legs spread wide, on the Seine's gentle shore,
Anchored deep, visitors always yearn for more.
Made of stiff iron, and groomed for a big fair,
Eiffel's creation, made romance fill the air.
It is admired for its shape, hardness, and height.
It was almost taken down, but folks said, "Not quite!"

The Panama Canal
Panama, 1914

Long ago, a waterway she was made,
Where big ships barged, and trade was laid.
Her water goes up and down, at a glance,
Connecting two oceans, like a mystical dance.
It made a shortcut, saving time and freight.
An inviting passage, letting men through its gates.
Captains must always, pull out before too late,
To let other eager seamen, have a chance to partake.

The Hoover Dam
USA, 1936

Between two places, a big erection did rise,
Holding back a huge load under blue skies.
In the desert, It's engorged, and it stands,
Pumping immense power, across her dry lands.
Its spillways gush, when things get too heated,
A marvel of control, never once defeated.
Its base is as thick, as two football fields wide,
With stats like that, it's any man's pride!

The Golden Gate Bridge
USA, 1937

In San Francisco, a curvy bridge stands,
Over the water, to far-off lands.
Spanning the bay, with legs firmly apart,
She's an art deco marvel and a work of art.
The bay fog caresses her arched shaped curves,
But to pass on her roads a big toll is served.
Each rivet and bolt, with a touch so precise,
With a firm grip makes her sturdy, so tight, and so nice.
Cars, bikes, and walkers, she welcomes them all,
With all passing on her, she spans ready, through it all.

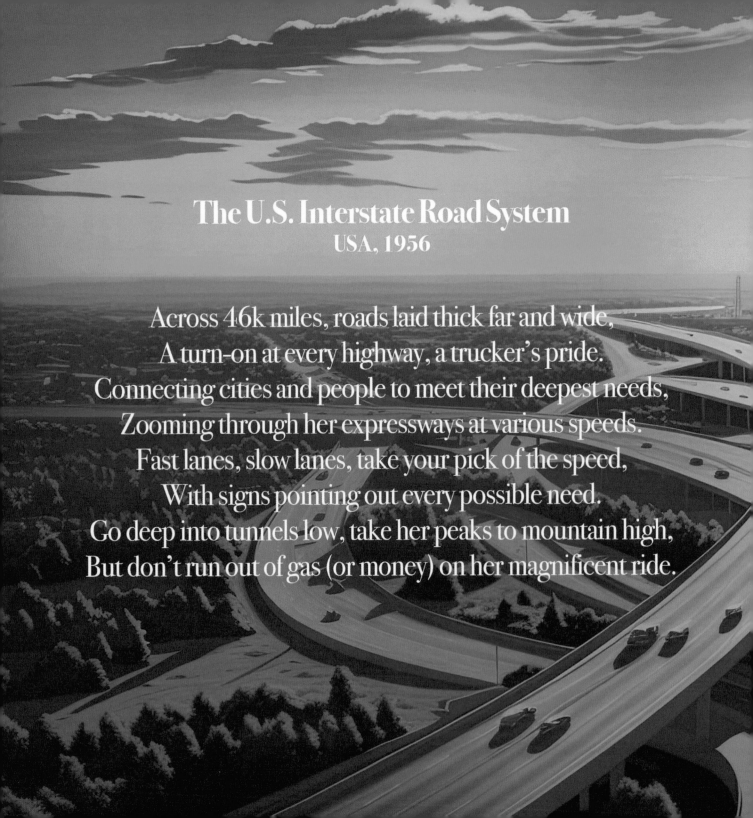

The U.S. Interstate Road System
USA, 1956

Across 46k miles, roads laid thick far and wide,
A turn-on at every highway, a trucker's pride.
Connecting cities and people to meet their deepest needs,
Zooming through her expressways at various speeds.
Fast lanes, slow lanes, take your pick of the speed,
With signs pointing out every possible need.
Go deep into tunnels low, take her peaks to mountain high,
But don't run out of gas (or money) on her magnificent ride.

The Gateway Arch
USA, 1965

In the heart of St. Louis, she stands proud and tall,
An engineering marvel, an erection for us all.
A perfect parabola, to behold, sense, and see,
As wide as she is tall, attests to perfect symmetry.
She beckons to the masses, with vast and open arms.
Flexible and curvy, with stainless steel charm,
Many dream of being inside her; to climax is what they seek,
To see the view around them within her stainless steel peak.
The view? Oh, it's ravishing, a sight for sorest eyes,
But watch your big heads, space might be a tight surprise!

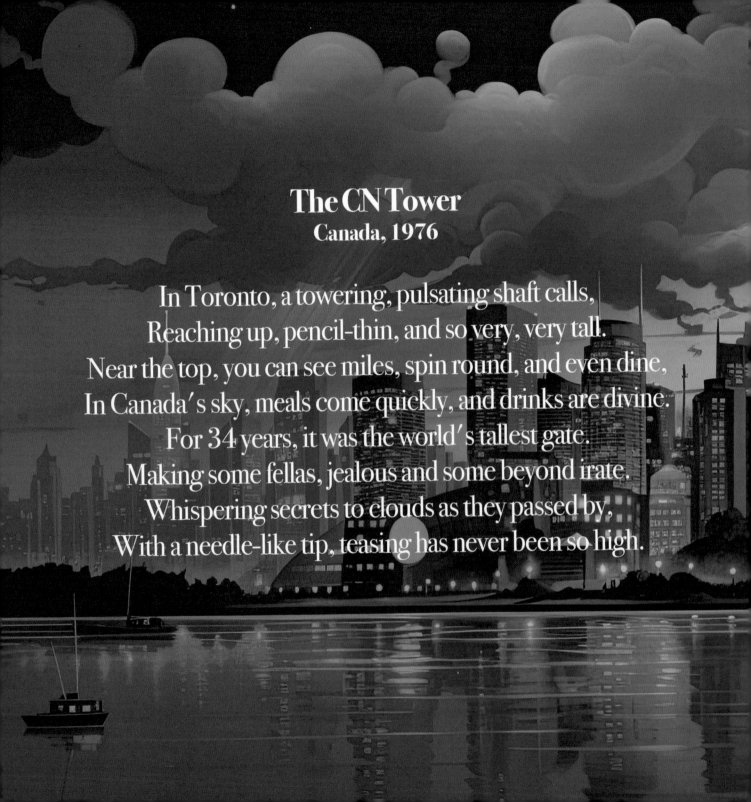

The CN Tower
Canada, 1976

In Toronto, a towering, pulsating shaft calls,
Reaching up, pencil-thin, and so very, very tall.
Near the top, you can see miles, spin round, and even dine,
In Canada's sky, meals come quickly, and drinks are divine.
For 34 years, it was the world's tallest gate,
Making some fellas, jealous and some beyond irate.
Whispering secrets to clouds as they passed by,
With a needle-like tip, teasing has never been so high.

The Sydney Opera House
Australia, 1973

By the water's bend, on Australia's breezy side,
Erections, like white sails, above the horizon rise.
Ships and crashing waves, emulate her shape.
Captains and other seamen, admire her wild seascape.
Against ocean blue, her cups are always showing,
An opera's magic place, her music is always flowing.
People from all the corners, come from near and wide,
Journey to gaze fondly at her majestic backside.
To hear her siren sound, to come inside her hall,
She entices, enchants, and envelops the freest of us all.

The International Space Station
Space, 1998

Amidst space's vast void, where stars often gleam,
The ISS floats by, an out-of-world dream.
Conception by nations, it took many, it's true,
A magnificent erection, with a cosmic view!
Modules come together, with precision, no deflection,
With every thrust and injection, perfect interconnection.
In this orbital ballet, desires are laid silent and bare,
A rendezvous in the cosmos, none else can compare.
Solar arrays spread wide, as they tilt with care,
Nations coming together, stellar intercourse to share.

The Burj Khalifa
UAE, 2010

A flowering Dubai tower, erected with manly might.
Piercing desert days, and supple moonlights.
Dominating the emerging skyline, so hard to ignore,
It invites temptation, promising a city at one door.
Its base, strong and sturdy, supports its enormous length,
A testament to its mammoth girth, and undeniable strength.
Getting to the top, you'll lose your breath, You'll never be higher,
Then, fondling the pointed tip, of the world's tallest spire!

With a tip of his hat and a sparkle in his gaze,
Willie addressed us all, his voice full of praise.

"From massive erections, that pierce the big blue sky,
To pulsating structures, that can leave us asking why?
Exploring erections through centuries, from pyramids, bridges, and more,
From canals, skyscrapers, and roadways, construction is at the core.
I hope you've learned a lesson, how exciting erections can be,
And hope you consider engineering to be more than just handy.

It's time to part, my dear friends, for this tale's end is near,
But worry not, for our adventures won't disappear.
Because today's structures are being built, even if still a surprise,
And our world can't wait for the next erection to come into our eyes.'

The End.

for now...

Hey Legend!

Book-writing is a grind, and we truly appreciate you not only buying this book, but hacking your way all the way through. Hopefully, you didn't upend any kid's birthday parties or religious gatherings!

The fun shouldn't stop here, and guess what? YOU hold the ticket to keep this steam-boat chugging.

Some quick ways to keep our dreams alive:

Rate This Beast
Drop a hilariously honest review on Amazon or your purchase point. Got writer's block? Boot up ChatGPT or Bard, and let the madness ensue. We'll be spotlighting the zaniest reviews on our socials. Let's make those critiques funnier than the book itself!

Prank & Delight Your Friends(or Enemies)
Noticed the QR Code? That's your gateway to more of our shenanigans. Ideal for those spontaneous giggle-bomb moments with friends or to send a clear message to someone you despise.

Feed Our Ramen Cravings
We've poured hours into this! Perhaps help us replenish our pantry with another instant noodle by snagging more of our reads. Same QR code works!

Steamily Yours,

The Cleaveland Steamer Press Crew

SCAN ME!

More hilarity by Cleveland Steamer Press

Our Friends & Parnters

Printed in Great Britain
by Amazon

35248712R00027